SCOOBY-DOO EXPLORES
CITIES

BY JOHN SAZAKLIS

PEBBLE
a capstone imprint

Published by Pebble, an imprint of Capstone
1710 Roe Crest Drive, North Mankato, Minnesota 56003
capstonepub.com

Library of Congress Cataloging-in-Publication Data is available on the Library of Congress website
ISBN: 9780756576493 (hardcover)
ISBN: 9780756576448 (paperback)
ISBN: 9780756576455 (ebook PDF)

Summary: Scooby-Doo and gang visit and learn about some well-known cities.

Editorial Credits
Editor: Christianne Jones; Designer: Bobbie Nuytten; Media Researcher: Rebekah Hubstenberger;
Production Specialist: Whitney Schaefer

Image Credits
Alamy: Reuters/David Gray, 26; Dreamstime: Ajacques2, 2 (bottom left), 8, Anna Krivitskaia,
10, Dennis Dolkens, 1, Jozef Sedmak, 13 (middle); Getty Images: Alexander Spatari, 12 (bottom),
14, 18, Alvin Huang, 29 (top left), Andrew Merry, 27 (middle), Archive Photos, 7 (top), Britus,
left), Hulton Archive, 11 (top middle), iStock/Ana maria Jimenez Benedetti, 21 (top right), iStock/
Andrew Bertuleit, 7 (bottom), iStock/Azulillo, 17 (top right), iStock/DarrenTierney, 27 (bottom),
iStock/Eliyahu Parypa, 4 (top right), iStock/gerenme, 7 (middle), iStock/IakovKalinin, 12 (top
right), iStock/Juanmonino, 6, iStock/Leonid Andronov, 3 (bottom left), 20, 23 (top), iStock/Luisa
Vallon Fumi, 31 (top), iStock/zrfphoto, 11 (middle left), Karl Hendon, 15 (top), Nikontiger, 29
(middle left), Sami Sarkis, 16, Yongyuan Dai, 31 (middle), Zsolt Hlinka, Cover (bottom right), 5
(middle right); NASA: JSC, 23 (bottom); Shutterstock: AfriramPOE, 3 (bottom right), 28, AlexAnton,
21 (middle), 22, 23 (middle), Bogdanov Oleg, 15 (bottom), Cedric Weber, 13 (top right), Claudio
Divizia, 15 (middle), DW labs Incorporated, 5 (middle left), Leah-Anne Thompson, 24 (top right),
Leonid Andronov, Cover (top right), Luciano Mortula - LGM, 31 (bottom), Maurizio De Mattei,
27 (top), Nataliya Hora, 30, nyker, 29 (top right), Photo Spirit, 9 (middle right), Ratov Maxim, 19
(bottom), S.Borisov, 9 (top right), saiko3p, 19 (middle, top), Taki O, 3 (bottom middle), 24 (bottom),
Taras Vyshnya, 25 (top, bottom right), travelview, 5 (top right), TTstudio, 17 (bottom left)

CITY SIGHTS

Scooby-Doo and Mystery Inc. are doing some big city sightseeing!

A city is a place where many people live and work. Most cities have tall buildings, big stores, and public transportation. They also have interesting landmarks and lots to do.

Use clues in the text and photos to guess which city the gang is exploring.

The Mystery Machine bounces over a bridge into this city on an island. From the harbor, the gang is greeted by the Statue of Liberty in all its green glory.

Soon they see the Empire State Building. It is a skyscraper with 102 floors. **JINKIES!**

Next they are wowed by the sights, sounds, and smells of the Broadway theater district in Times Square.

SCOOBY-DOO, WHERE ARE YOU?

WE ARE IN NEW YORK CITY!

Like, it's always time to eat in the city that never sleeps.

Rummy in my tummy!

New York City was the first capital of the United States.

The NYC subway system is the largest in the world. It has nearly 500 stations!

Central Park is in the center of the city. It has lakes, ponds, ice-skating rinks, a carousel, and a zoo!

The next city Scooby and the gang visit also has a park in its center.

It is called the National Mall, but you can't go shopping. It has a famous Reflecting Pool, but you can't go swimming.

On either end of the park is the Washington Monument and the Lincoln Memorial. These structures honor past U.S. presidents.

And speaking of presidents, the current one lives here at the White House. **GROOVY!**

SCOOBY-DOO, WHERE ARE YOU?

WE ARE IN WASHINGTON, D.C.!

Smithsonian's National Air and Space Museum has the most airplanes and spacecraft in the world. It is one of many museums in Washington, D.C.

George Washington was the first U.S. president.

He also had false teeth.

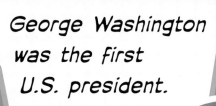

Like, were they called presidentures?

Ree-hee-hee-hee!

Washington, D.C. became the United States capital in 1790.

The three branches of federal government are in Washington, D.C. They include the legislative, executive, and judicial branch.

The members of Mystery Inc. can see this city from the Tower Bridge on the River Thames.

GONG! They hear the bell of the clock tower nicknamed Big Ben.

Time to reach new heights! The fun-loving friends find Europe's tallest Ferris wheel.

And there's Buckingham Palace, home of the royal family and their distinguished doggies.

SCOOBY-DOO, WHERE ARE YOU?

WE ARE IN LONDON!

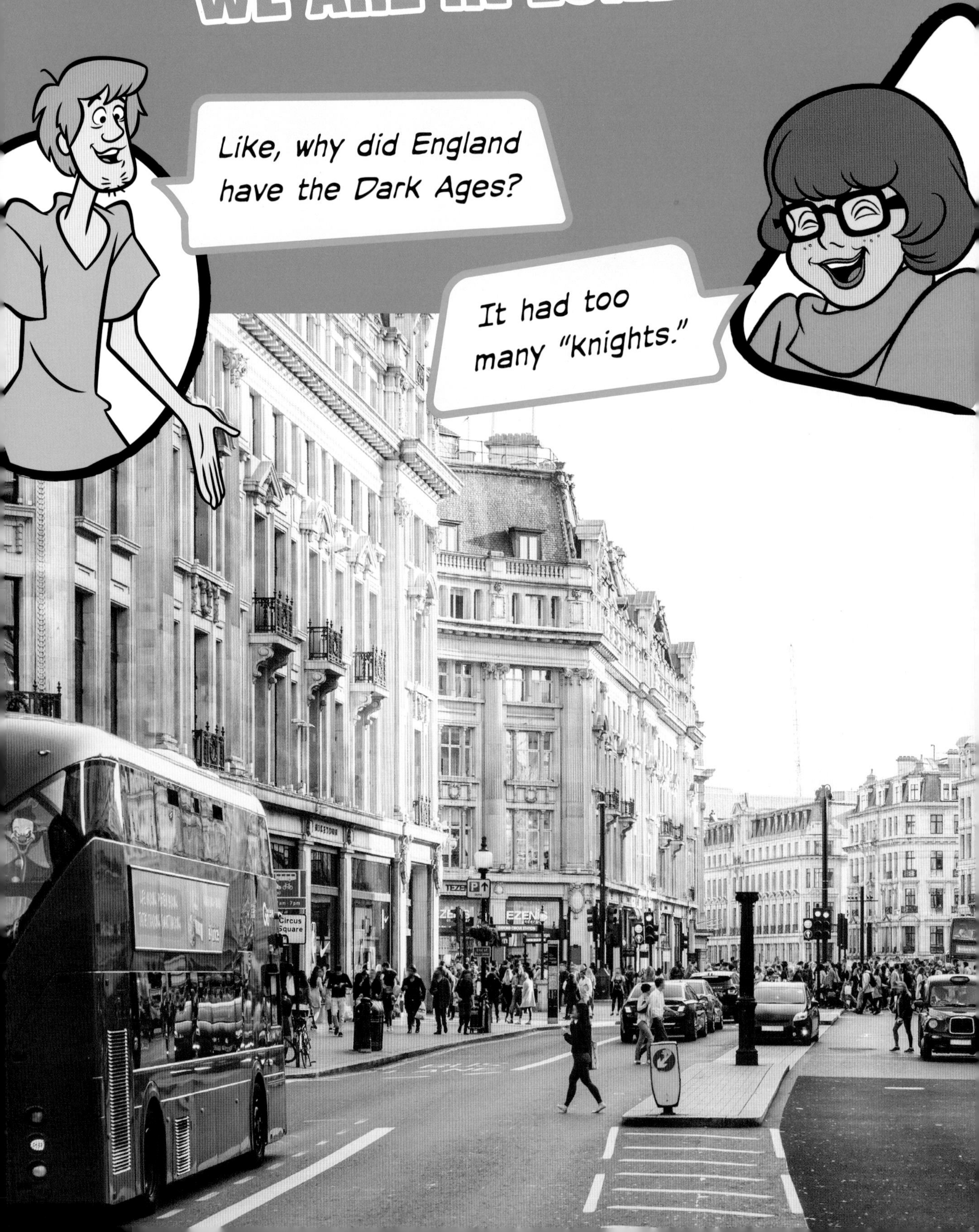

London is the capital and largest city of England.

London was founded by the Romans in 47 CE and called Londinium.

The Tower of London once had a pet polar bear that would catch fish in the River Thames.

Scooby-Doo and friends find the "City of Light." They see its bright beacon, the Eiffel Tower, shining.

They visit the Louvre. It is the most popular art museum in the world and also the largest!

Then the gang poses with the Arc de Triomphe. It is also known as the Arch of Victory.

And finally, there's Notre-Dame—a stunning gothic cathedral that is said to be haunted. **ZOINKS!**

SCOOBY-DOO, WHERE ARE YOU?

WE ARE IN PARIS!

Like, why do French restaurants have snails on the menu?

Because they don't serve "fast" food.

Paris is the capital of France and is divided in two by the Seine River.

There are 1,665 steps from the base of the Eiffel Tower to the very top.

Snails are a popular dish in Paris. Around 40,000 tons of snails are eaten every year in France.

The gang takes a stand atop of the Citadel of Saladin on this hot, humid desert day.

Scooby and Shaggy want to dive into the Nile River and cool off.

Jeepers! The Great Pyramid of Giza was once the crypt of many mummies. And the Great Sphinx looks like a mystical, mythical monster.

SCOOBY-DOO, WHERE ARE YOU?

Cairo is the capital of Egypt and the largest city in Africa.

The Pyramid of Giza is a tomb for the pharaoh Khufu. It took about 100,000 men and around 20 years to build.

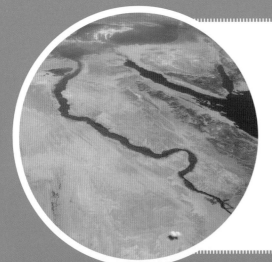

Cairo is built next to the Nile, which is one of the longest rivers on Earth.

The Mystery Machine treks over the Harbour Bridge in the next city on their list.

The buildings of this city are dwarfed by the Blue Mountains.

Scooby-Doo and the gang take a stroll on Bondi Beach, which covers almost 3.5 miles (5.6 kilometers) along the coast.

The Sydney Opera House sits on the water. It has an iconic design.

SCOOBY-DOO, WHERE ARE YOU?

WE ARE IN SYDNEY!

Like, what's your favorite instrument, Scoob?

Rhat's easy. It's the Scooby-Didgeri-Doo!

didgeridoo

Sydney is the capital of New South Wales, a state in the country of Australia.

The best-known attraction of the Blue Mountains is a rock formation called The Three Sisters.

Sydney has more than 100 beaches!

Scooby and the group zoom into a new city by way of the Shinkansen bullet train. **Whoosh!**

This tech-savvy city is a combination of the future and the past. Check out the centuries-old Imperial Palace and the sleek Skytree Tower.

Visible on the horizon is Mount Fuji, which is an active volcano. *ZOINKS!*

SCOOBY-DOO, WHERE ARE YOU?

WE ARE IN TOKYO!

In Electric Town, you're surely in for a shock!

Ruh-roh!

30

Before Tokyo became the capital of Japan in 1868, it was a fishing village called Edo.

Akihabara (also known as Electric Town) is a busy shopping area. It is popular area for fans of anime, manga, and games.

There are more neon signs in Tokyo than anywhere else in the world.

Scooby-Doo and the Mystery Inc. gang traveled all over the world, but they weren't alone! Ghost Clown wanted to do some fright-seeing! Look through the book again and find him hiding in each city.

ABOUT THE AUTHOR

John Sazaklis is a *New York Times* bestselling author with almost 100 children's books under his utility belt! He has also illustrated Spider-Man books, created toys for MAD magazine, and written for the BEN 10 animated series. John lives in New York City with his superpowered wife and daughter.